P9-ARP-777

EMMA S. CLARK MEMORIAL LIBRARY
Setauket, L.I., New York 11733

KINGFISHER KNOWLEDGE

SHARKS

▼ Sharks are the ocean's main predators.
This blue shark has a typical streamlined shape.

SHARKS

Miranda Smith

Foreword by
Valerie Taylor

KINGFISHER
NEW YORK

KINGFISHER
LONDON & NEW YORK

Consultant: David Burnie

Copyright © 2008 by Kingfisher
Published in the United States by Kingfisher,
175 Fifth Ave., New York, NY 10010
Kingfisher is an imprint of Macmillan Children's Books, London.
All rights reserved.

Distributed in the U.S. by Macmillan, 175 Fifth Ave., New York, NY 10010
Distributed in Canada by H.B. Fenn and Company Ltd., .
34 Nixon Road, Bolton, Ontario L7E 1W2

LIBRARY OF CONGRESS CATALOGING-IN-PUBLICATION DATA
Smith, Miranda.
    Sharks / Miranda Smith. -- 1st ed.
        p. cm. -- (Kingfisher knowledge)
    Includes index.
    ISBN 978-0-7534-6194-5
    1. Sharks--Juvenile literature. I. Title
    QL638.9.S58 2008
    597.3--dc22
            2007030937

ISBN 978-0-7534-6194-5

Kingfisher books are available for special promotions and premiums. For details contact:
Special Markets Department, Macmillan,
175 Fifth Avenue,
New York, NY 10010.

For more information, please visit
www.kingfisherpublications.com

Printed in Singapore
10 9 8 7 6 5 4 3 2

2TR/0209/TWP/MA(MA)/
130ENSOMA/F

503 6411

Contents

NOTE TO READERS
The web site addresses listed in this book are correct at the time of going to print. However, due to the ever-changing nature of the Internet, web site addresses and content can change. Web sites can contain links that are unsuitable for children. The publisher cannot be held responsible for changes in web site addresses or content or for information obtained through third-party web sites. We strongly advise that Internet searches are supervised by an adult.

▼ A blue shark is filmed in the ocean off the coast of California.

GO FURTHER . . .
INFORMATION PANEL KEY:

web sites and further reading

career paths

places to visit

Foreword

The shark is a rare and beautiful animal, so perfect in design that it has not changed in millions of years. It is also an animal I've worked with for most of my adult life. On page 54, you can see me in the water with a whitetip reef shark. My husband, cameraman Ron Taylor, and I have made a successful career by specializing in filming sharks. You can read about shark movies on pages 50–51.

Probably our best-known footage was shot for the film *Jaws*, but my most dramatic moment happened while working on a documentary called *Amazing Animals*. We were filming 60 mi. (100km) off the coast of San Diego, California. We had used bait to attract dozens of blue sharks, just like the ones on pages 26–27. Perhaps because there were so many of them, they seemed unusually excited; I was busy punching them away when I felt a thump on my left leg. Looking down, I saw a good-sized shark with my leg in its mouth. I grabbed its nose and tried to push it off. On my fourth hit I finally saw its teeth pull back from my leg. I didn't feel pain or fear—just annoyance that the shark had been so persistent. Blood clouded the water. I tried to stop it, but my middle finger sank from sight into the wound. *I'm going to bleed to death*, I thought. I tried without success to pull the thick neoprene of my wetsuit over the gash. Then someone was helping me get through the sharks back to the boat—I don't remember too well. The coast guard, already in the air, arrived in minutes. I was taken by helicopter to the hospital, where it took 300 stitches to sew my leg back together. Yes, it did become painful—very painful—and it still gives me trouble, but my own quick thinking saved my leg. I have been bitten twice more, but not badly. If I make the decision to enter the domain of a predator and things go wrong, it's entirely my fault. Mercifully, as you will see on pages 40–41, shark attacks are relatively rare.

Another of my most memorable shark encounters was with a species that is rarely seen—the great hammerhead. (You can read about hammerheads on pages 18–19.) To hang in the open water and watch a 20-ft. (6-m)-long shark emerge from the gloom, its enormous head swinging back and forth, makes one's heart jump. To have the same beast swim directly toward you and look you over—not once, but many times—makes you feel like exactly what you are: an out-of-place earthling in an alien environment. There was no threat, just curiosity, but it was still unsettling. The shark was so very big, with such long, sharp teeth, and its expressionless eyes seemed to be boring into mine. Eventually, curiosity satisfied, the hammerhead disappeared just as silently as it had arrived.

I hope that one day you will have the opportunity to get up close to sharks in the water as I have done. In the meantime, you can observe them and learn about them by reading this book. As you will read on pages 56–57, spreading knowledge about sharks is one of the most important ways that we can help protect them.

Valerie Taylor

Valerie Taylor, shark expert and marine conservationist

CHAPTER 1

Meet the shark

A powerful and determined hunter scything through the waves, the shark's jaws widen to reveal terrifying, razor-sharp teeth. Is this the picture that springs to mind when the word *shark* is mentioned? Despite their reputation, most sharks are harmless and shark attacks are very rare. Sharks probably have more to fear from humans than vice versa. Of all the animals that have existed on Earth, there are not many that have been around as long, or survived as well, as the shark. The ancestors of this skillful predator were swimming in the oceans 450 million years ago— 220 million years before the age of the dinosaurs even began. Today there are around 375 species of sharks. Sharks are found all over the world, from tropical seas to cold polar waters and from the ocean depths to estuaries and rivers.

An oceanic whitetip shark swims in the tropical seas off Hawaii, accompanied by striped pilot fish.

The shark family

A typical shark has a sleek, streamlined shape. Its body tapers off at both ends, allowing the shark to glide smoothly through the water without using a lot of energy. Most sharks never stop swimming and can only move forward. A shark also never sleeps. It has superb senses that it uses to avoid predators and find prey. And a shark has no bones—instead, its skeleton is made of cartilage, a tough, flexible tissue made of fibers.

All shapes and sizes

Sharks range in size from the massive whale shark to the tiny pygmy shark (see pages 16–17). They vary a lot in shape as well. Angel sharks and wobbegongs have flattened bodies, hammerheads have unusually wide heads, while frilled sharks are long and eel-like. Some sharks, such as mako sharks and tiger sharks, are swift hunters. Others, including the zebra bullhead shark, search the seabed for crabs and clams. And some, such as the basking shark, filter plankton from the water.

mouth is under snout

eye has nictitating membrane (inner eyelid)

gill slits

snout is long and pointed

nostril is used for smelling, not breathing

pectoral fin lifts shark as it swims

◀ Sharks, rays, and skates all belong to a class of fish called Chondrichthyes, the cartilaginous fishes. Sharks consist of around 375 species. Scientists group them into eight orders according to the physical characteristics that they share.

SHARK FAMILY TREE

flattened body

SQUATINIFORMES (angel sharks)

no anal fin

long snout

PRISTIOPHORIFORMES (sawsharks)

rounded body

(sleeper sharks
SQUALIFORMES and dogfish)

short snout

HEXANCHIFORMES (cow sharks)

1 dorsal fin; 6–7 gill slits

nictitating membranes (inner eyelids)
CARCHARHINIFORMES (ground sharks)

mouth behind eyes

anal fin

no spines on dorsal fin

LAMNIFORMES (mackerel sharks)
no nictitating membranes (inner eyelids)

ORECTOLOBIFORMES (carpet sharks)

mouth in front of eyes

2 dorsal fins; 5 gill slits

HETERODONTIFORMES (bullhead sharks)

spines on dorsal fin

On the move

All sharks swim by moving their heads from side to side. This movement spreads down the body in waves, becoming more exaggerated as it reaches the caudal (tail) fin. The push of the tail against the water thrusts the shark forward. At the same time, water flows over the pectoral and pelvic fins, which are shaped like aircraft wings—rounded at the front and sharp-edged at the back. This generates lift and stops the shark from sinking. To move in different directions, the shark tilts its fins.

dorsal fin acts like a stabilizer and stops shark from rolling

crescent-shaped caudal fin propels shark forward

anal fin stabilizes shark as it swims

pelvic fin helps shark swim in a level position

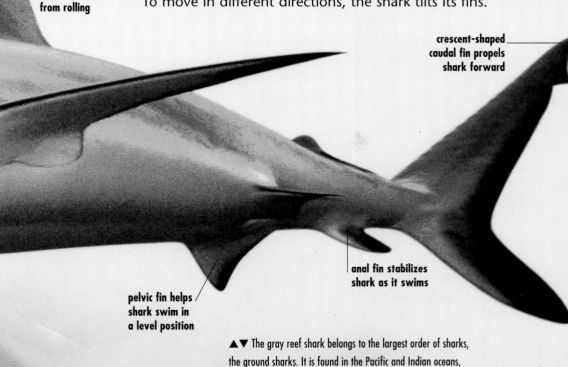

▲▼ The gray reef shark belongs to the largest order of sharks, the ground sharks. It is found in the Pacific and Indian oceans, often near coral reefs. Its white underside and gray back are a type of camouflage known as countershading. Seen from above, the gray blends in with the dark water below. Seen from underneath, the white blends in with the sea's sunlit surface.

▲ This close-up shows how sharkskin is dotted with tiny scales called denticles. They reduce drag, but rubbed the wrong way, denticles make the skin feel as rough as sandpaper. As a shark grows, its old denticles fall off and new ones take their place.

▲ These three rows of sawlike teeth belong to a great white shark. Sharks often lose teeth when killing and eating prey. As a tooth breaks off or wears down, another rotates forward to take its place. Sharks can lose as many as 30,000 teeth in a lifetime.

▲ Like most sharks, this basking shark has five pairs of gill slits, or openings, on both sides of its head. As the shark swims, water flows through its mouth, pushes across its gills, and is then expelled through the gill slits. The gills filter oxygen from the water.

Inside a shark

Like all animals, a shark needs to breathe, move, and eat. Its anatomy (body structure) has evolved to do all of these things efficiently. A shark "breathes" through gills that take in oxygen from the water. It moves easily through the water because the cartilage that forms its skeleton is lighter than bone and helps it float. Its digestive system allows it to feed on sea creatures, such as other fish, shellfish, or mammals, and to absorb the nutrients that they contain.

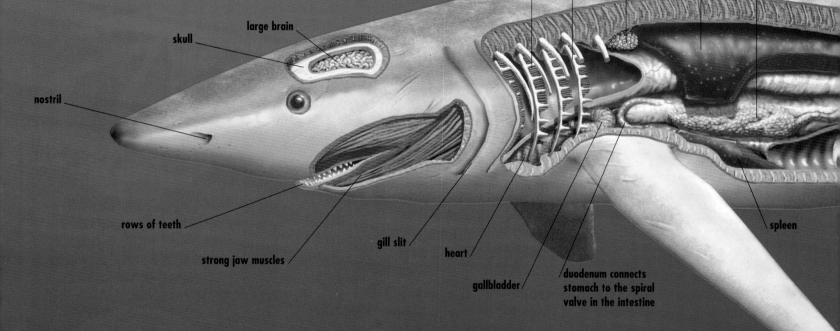

gill raker, like a tooth of a comb

gill arch

ovary and eggs

pancreas aids digestion

large liver provides buoyancy

large brain

skull

nostril

rows of teeth

strong jaw muscles

gill slit

heart

gallbladder

duodenum connects stomach to the spiral valve in the intestine

spleen

SHARK TAIL SHAPES

Great white sharks have crescent-shaped, symmetrical tail lobes. By controlling the speed at which the tail moves from side to side, they can switch from slow cruising to fast sprinting.

Tiger sharks have tails with a very long upper lobe and relatively short bottom lobe. Their asymmetric tails are good for twisting and turning, as well as for accelerating quickly when chasing prey.

Nurse sharks are bottom feeders that spend most of their time traveling like eels along the seabed. They do not need to accelerate suddenly, so the bottom lobe has almost completely disappeared.

Cookie-cutter sharks have tails with broad lobes that are almost the same size. This shape is not good for fast swimming, but that does not matter. The lobes are bioluminescent and lure prey toward the shark.

Energetic food processors

Sharks are successful hunters and determined feeders. They need to be, as they must eat up to three percent of their body weight each day in order to survive. Their intestine is short and straight—a design that would normally let food pass through too quickly to be absorbed properly. However, sharks are also equipped with a valve—in a spiral, ring, or scroll shape—that is lined with folds of membranes that slow digestion.

Staying afloat

Sharks do not have gas-filled swim bladders like bony fish, and most will sink if they stop swimming, but their very large liver helps keep them afloat. The liver has two large lobes (rounded parts) that store fats and an oil called squalene. This oil is what helps sharks float, because it is lighter than water. The fats and squalene are also a supply of energy. If a shark does not find enough to eat, it metabolizes the fats and squalene (chemically changes them into energy) to sustain itself until it finds food.

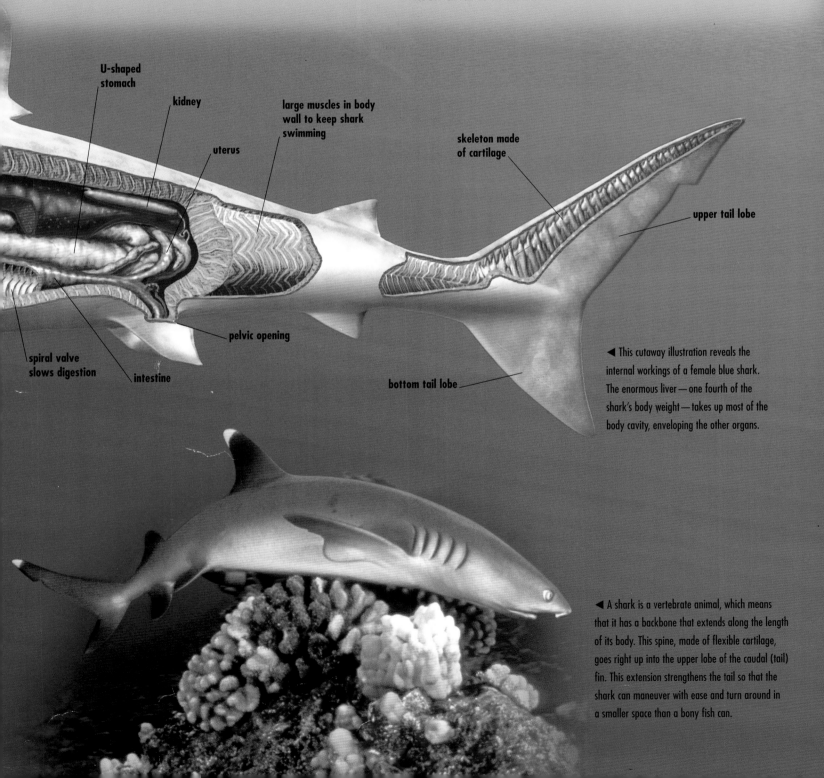

U-shaped stomach

kidney

large muscles in body wall to keep shark swimming

uterus

skeleton made of cartilage

upper tail lobe

spiral valve slows digestion

pelvic opening

intestine

bottom tail lobe

◄ This cutaway illustration reveals the internal workings of a female blue shark. The enormous liver — one fourth of the shark's body weight — takes up most of the body cavity, enveloping the other organs.

◄ A shark is a vertebrate animal, which means that it has a backbone that extends along the length of its body. This spine, made of flexible cartilage, goes right up into the upper lobe of the caudal (tail) fin. This extension strengthens the tail so that the shark can maneuver with ease and turn around in a smaller space than a bony fish can.

Giving birth

Around one third of sharks—including wobbegongs, catsharks, and horn sharks—are oviparous, which means that they reproduce by laying eggs. Like birds, bony fish, and some reptiles, they lay fertilized eggs that are surrounded by a shell. The shells are soft while the eggs are in the uterus, but they harden in the water, forming a protective case around the embryo. There are two other ways that sharks reproduce: giving birth to live young (viviparity) and producing eggs that hatch inside the body (ovoviviparity).

Viviparous sharks

Most of the sharks that give birth to live young are larger species such as lemon, blue, and hammerhead sharks. The embryos develop inside the uterus in a similar way to how human babies and other mammals grow. At first they feed on stored yolk. Later, they get oxygen and nutrients from their mother through a placenta, along an umbilical cord that also takes waste away. When they are fully developed, the shark pups are born live.

▼ A small-spotted catshark pup swims out of its egg case. Its mother laid the egg six to 12 months earlier and then swam away and left the pup to develop on its own. Egg cases often wash up on beaches and are nicknamed mermaids' purses.

Ovoviviparous sharks

Most sharks, including sand tigers, great whites, and spiny dogfish, reproduce by ovoviviparity. The embryos develop in a shell-like case inside the uterus. When they are mature, they hatch inside the female, which gives birth to live pups. The embryos are not connected by a placenta to the mother; instead they feed on yolk stored inside a yolk sac. In the case of the sand tiger, the first embryo to use up its yolk becomes a cannibal, eating up the remaining embryos and any unfertilized eggs.

▶ This newborn spiny dogfish developed ovoviviparously as an egg inside its mother's uterus. It is still attached to its yolk sac. Spiny dogfish have the longest-known gestation period of any shark—around 22 months—and produce litters of up to 16 pups. At birth they measure around 10 in. (25cm), almost one fourth of their adult length.

▼ A lemon shark's pregnancy lasts from ten to 12 months. When it is ready to give birth, the shark swims into sheltered, coastal waters. Its litter may contain up to 17 pups. Each pup rests for a moment on the seabed and then swims away, breaking the umbilical cord. It will stay in its birth area for the first few years of its life.

Ancient sharks

Most prehistoric sharks were very different from the sharks in today's oceans, but they were still recognizably sharks. Few complete shark fossils have been found because cartilage does not survive well, but there is plenty of fossil evidence in the form of teeth, scales, and fin spines. The earliest shark fossils are in rocks that are 400 million years old.

▲ One of the strangest of the early sharks was the 6.5-ft. (2-m)-long *Stethacanthus*, which swam in the oceans more than 360 million years ago (m.y.a). Its anvil-shaped dorsal fin looks like an open mouth and may have evolved to attract mates or to frighten off predators.

Fossil evidence

In October 1666, a Danish doctor named Nicolas Steno made a discovery that changed history. He was dissecting the head of a large shark, caught off the coast of Italy, when he realized that he had seen the teeth somewhere else. For centuries, *glossopetrae* ("tongue stones") had been used in courts throughout Europe as magical amulets. Steno recognized that *glossopetrae* were not snakes' tongues, as people had thought, but fossilized sharks' teeth. His findings marked the birth of a new science: paleontology.

▶ *Megalodon* ("big tooth"), a shark that lived from 25 to 5 m.y.a., seizes its whale prey in its 6-in. (15-cm)-long teeth. One of the most formidable predators ever to have swum in the oceans, *Megalodon* measured up to 49 ft. (15m) long—around twice the size of a great white shark.

The first "modern" sharks

Around 350 million years ago (m.y.a.), prehistoric sharks began to split into different groups that had different characteristics. The ancestors of modern sharks appeared around 200 m.y.a. at the beginning of the Jurassic period, when dinosaurs roamed Earth. Most of the shark groups that swim in the oceans today—including bullhead, goblin, sand, nurse, cow, and angel sharks—evolved during this period. Great white sharks appeared at least 65 m.y.a.

▶ This photograph shows part of an extraordinary fossil—a spiral of teeth from the jaw of a shark called *Helicoprion* that lived 280 to 225 m.y.a. The fossil contains at least 180 teeth, with the oldest teeth on the outside, pushed there by the most recently formed teeth in the middle of the spiral.

▼ These fossil shark teeth are embedded in a rock that is 40 million years old. They belonged to a prehistoric member of the mackerel shark family, which includes today's salmon sharks and porbeagles.

Record breakers

The oceans' watery depths are home to an incredible variety of sharks, each with habits and abilities that have evolved to fit in with its particular habitat and lifestyle. The shark family includes the biggest fish in the ocean, the whale shark, as well as some of the fastest, mako sharks and porbeagles. Shark life spans vary enormously, too. Some species live for only 20 or 30 years, but others, such as the spiny dogfish, may reach 100 years old.

▲ This pygmy shark is around half its adult size. Mature females grow to around 9 in. (24cm) long, and males are even smaller at as little as 7 in. (17cm). The pygmy shark feeds close to the water's surface at night, but moves to a depth of around 5,250 ft. (1,600m) during the day. Its underside glows as it swims.

Smallest of all

There are several contenders for the title of smallest shark. Most spined pygmy sharks are 8–10 in. (20–25cm), but a mature male shark has been measured at only 6 in. (15cm) long. The dwarf dogfish is a mere 6–9 in. (16–22cm), while the dwarf lanternshark, which glows in the dark depths of the deep oceans, only reaches around 8 in. (20cm). One female pygmy ribbontail catshark was a tiny 7 in. (18cm) long.

Giant sharks

At 49 ft. (15m) long, the whale shark is the largest fish on Earth. Its cavernous mouth is 5 ft. (1.5m) across—large enough for a car to be driven inside it. The whale shark is a filter feeder (see pages 42–43). It swims along with its mouth wide open, scooping up krill, squids, and small fish such as sardines and anchovies. The 30-ft. (10-m)-long basking shark, also a filter feeder, is the second-largest shark. Its vast jaw may be up to 3 ft. (1m) wide.

▼ A whale shark cruises close to the surface. It is as big as a humpback whale and weighs up to 15 tons—the same as three elephants. Its liver alone may weigh one ton. Whale sharks also hold the record for having the most pups at one time—several hundred in one litter.

▲ The fastest shark is probably the shortfin mako. It cuts through the water at 30 mph (50km/h) and may even top 45 mph (75km/h) in short bursts while chasing fast-moving fish and squids. The mako can also leap 20 ft. (6m) out of the water to make a quick getaway from a fishing line.

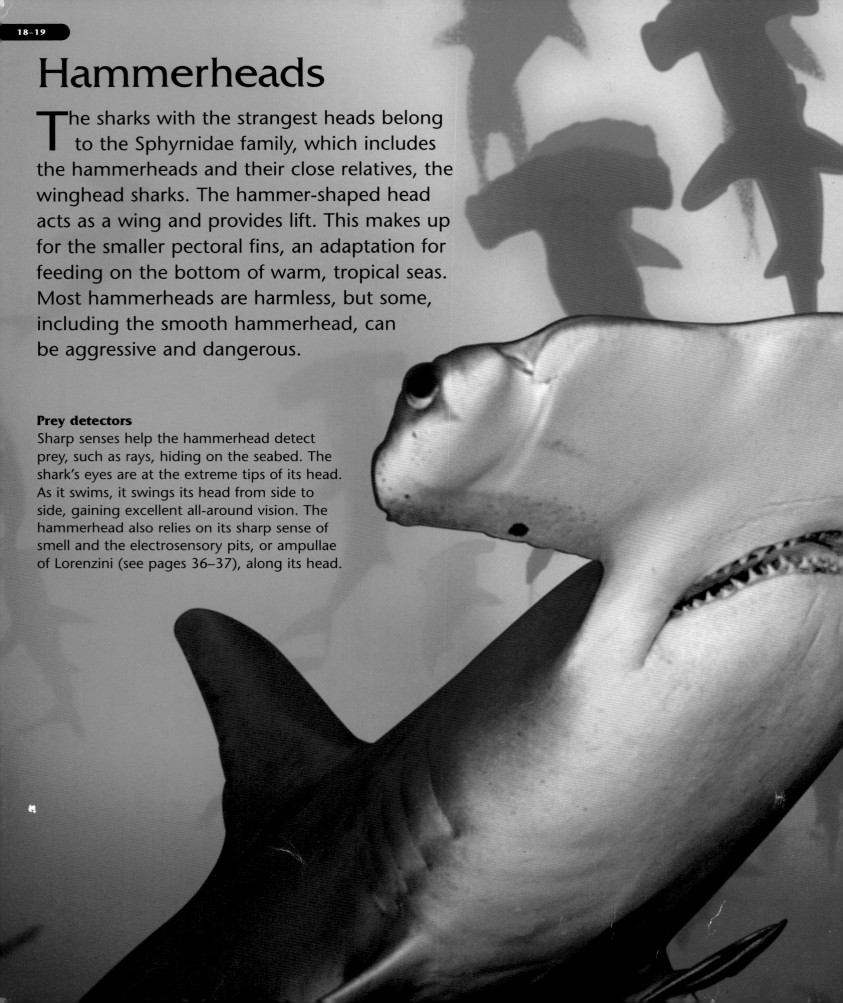

Hammerheads

The sharks with the strangest heads belong to the Sphyrnidae family, which includes the hammerheads and their close relatives, the winghead sharks. The hammer-shaped head acts as a wing and provides lift. This makes up for the smaller pectoral fins, an adaptation for feeding on the bottom of warm, tropical seas. Most hammerheads are harmless, but some, including the smooth hammerhead, can be aggressive and dangerous.

Prey detectors

Sharp senses help the hammerhead detect prey, such as rays, hiding on the seabed. The shark's eyes are at the extreme tips of its head. As it swims, it swings its head from side to side, gaining excellent all-around vision. The hammerhead also relies on its sharp sense of smell and the electrosensory pits, or ampullae of Lorenzini (see pages 36–37), along its head.

Scalloped hammerheads

Scalloped hammerheads often gather in very large groups of up to 500 at one time. They are the only sharks to do this, coming together by day and breaking away to feed on their own at night. Most of the individuals are females, so perhaps they are gathering where males can find them easily or to protect their young. Or the sharks may be seeking safety in numbers, like schooling fish, to confuse predatory great white sharks, tiger sharks, or killer whales.

◄ The distinctive hammer-shaped head of the scalloped hammerhead has a deep indentation in the middle. The hammer measures 23–35 in. (60–90cm) wide, which is roughly one fourth of the shark's body length.

◄ At 20 ft. (6m) long, the great hammerhead is the largest member of the hammerhead family. It is also an aggressive hunter. It pins down stingrays with its head while biting off the rays' wings.

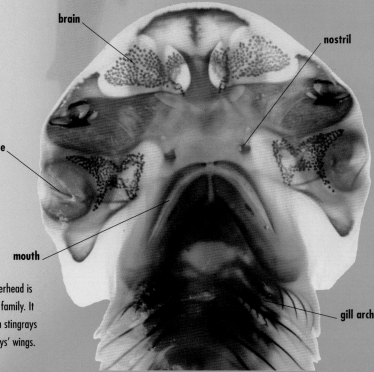

brain

nostril

eye

mouth

gill arch

▲ This transparent specimen of a bonnethead shark shows in blue the cartilage that forms the shape of its head, with its eyes at either end. The gill arches are beneath the jaws.

HEAD SHAPES

The great hammerhead is one of the world's largest predatory fish. Sometimes found in water only 3 ft. (1m) deep, it uses its wide head to stir up sand on the seabed in order to find prey.

The scalloped hammerhead has four graceful lobes on the edge of its head. It is the most common hammerhead, often found close to the shore in warm seas, bays, and estuaries.

The bonnethead has a broad, shovel-like head. It is the smallest hammerhead, around 3 ft. (1m) long. Its main food is crustaceans, which it crushes with the large molars at the back of its jaw.

The winghead shark has the widest head in the family relative to its size. Its body is around 3 ft. (1m) long, but its head may be 20 in. (50cm) across. The large nostrils are almost twice the width of the mouth.

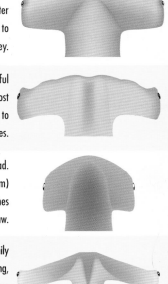

Rarest of all

In January 1998, researchers reported sighting a rare Borneo river shark for the first time in 100 years. If sharks are described as "rare," it usually means that they are seldom seen. The majority of species that are classified as rare live in the deep oceans, where they are unlikely to be spotted. Others, such as the whitetip soupfin and the great white, are rare because people have killed so many that they have become endangered.

Deep-water monsters
One of the most extraordinary of the rarely seen deep-sea sharks is the megamouth, named for its enormous 3-ft. (1-m)-wide mouth. The first one was found off Hawaii in 1976; during the following 30 years, only 38 were seen. The Greenland shark is another rare shark. It is found at depths of up to 1,800 ft. (550m) in chilly Arctic waters and only comes close to the surface during the winter months. A slow swimmer, it probably ambushes its fast-moving fish prey.

▼ The Greenland shark hunts in darkness underneath the Arctic ice, using its sharp sense of smell to find food. Most Greenland sharks have been blinded by parasites called copepods, which attach themselves to the corneas in the sharks' eyes. The copepods glow in the gloom and may attract prey for the shark.

A living fossil

An extraordinary shark was first identified off eastern Japan in 1898. Japanese fishermen called it *tenguzame*, meaning "goblin shark." It is an example of a living fossil because it is the only surviving member of a family that has been around for 100 million years—its teeth resemble those of the prehistoric shark *Scapanorhyncus*. The goblin shark lives on the seabed at depths of 1,150–4,000 ft. (350–1,200m). It feeds on squids and small fish.

▲ The goblin shark's long snout may contain electrosensory canals (ampullae of Lorenzini) that help the shark detect prey. Once it has tracked down its quarry, the shark's jaws shoot forward to snap it up.

▼ Sawsharks and their relatives, sawfish, have suffered greatly from habitat loss, overfishing, and hunting for their "saws," which have become collectors' items. This 23-ft. (7-m)-long smalltooth sawfish is one of two species that lives in U.S. waters. It uses its saw to wound and kill as it charges at schools of fish and also to dig in the sediment for crabs and shellfish.

Close relatives

Rays, skates, guitarfish, and sawfish look very different from sharks, but they are closely related. Like sharks, they have skeletons made out of cartilage instead of bone. They also have gill slits, although these are on the undersides of their bodies. Unlike sharks, they have flattened pectoral fins that stick out from their heads like wings.

Underwater fliers

There is no sight more graceful than the largest ray of all, the 23-ft. (7-m)-wide manta, gracefully flapping its pectoral fins. It looks like a strange bird in flight as it glides along. Rays and skates travel through the water in a completely different way than sharks. Torpedo rays send ripples along their bodies that propel them forward. Leg skates have lobes (rounded pieces of skin) on their pelvic fins that they use to "kick" themselves along.

▶ Spotted eagle rays swim in warm coastal waters, sometimes in large schools. They use their beaklike snouts to search in the mud for shellfish. Sometimes, when they are being hunted by predators such as silvertip and great hammerhead sharks, they can leap up out of the water.

▶ The common skate is a 10-ft. (3-m)-long predator, armed with up to 18 poisonous thorns along its tail. It feeds on crabs, lobsters, and bottom-dwelling fish in deep European waters. Like many rays and skates, it is threatened by overfishing. Despite its name, the common skate is critically endangered.

Sting in the tail

Rays and skates use a variety of weapons. Many rays have poisonous spines on their whiplike tails that can stun or kill prey and most predators (but not sharks). Electric rays may send an electrical current of more than 200 volts through the water—strong enough to stun the fish and crabs that they eat. The sawfish (see page 21) has a saw-shaped jaw for slashing at prey and defending itself against predators. Another distant relative, the chimera, is armed with a venomous spine on its dorsal fin.

▼ A young snorkeler reaches out to touch a southern stingray in the Caribbean Sea. This stingray cruises over coral reefs, stopping to dig in the sandy patches for mollusks and crustaceans. It is also an ambush predator, lying camouflaged on the sandy seabed until it can surprise passing small fish or other prey.

Migration

Sharks sometimes travel long distances, but it is only recently that new technology, such as satellite tagging, has made it possible to track them. Some sharks migrate to mate and produce young in the best possible conditions. Others cross the oceans to find or follow food. Basking sharks also migrate vertically, moving between the surface and the ocean depths, depending on where plankton is most plentiful.

Incredible distances

Every year, female blue sharks feed and mate off the east coast of North America and head almost 1,900 mi. (3,000km) across the Atlantic Ocean to give birth off the coast of Africa. Tiger sharks also travel widely in the North Atlantic Ocean, sometimes reaching South America or Africa. Bull sharks have been found an amazing 2,600 mi. (4,200km) up the Amazon River in the foothills of the Andes Mountains in Peru.

North Atlantic Ocean

North America

blue shark

Pacific Ocean

tiger shark

equator

bull shark

South America

South Atlantic Ocean

◄ Satellite tracking of tiger sharks has shown that they migrate to take advantage of different food sources. Some travel long distances to reach the coast of Hawaii each year when the albatross chicks hatch there. Tiger sharks have also been tracked to Raine Island, off eastern Australia, during the turtle-nesting season.

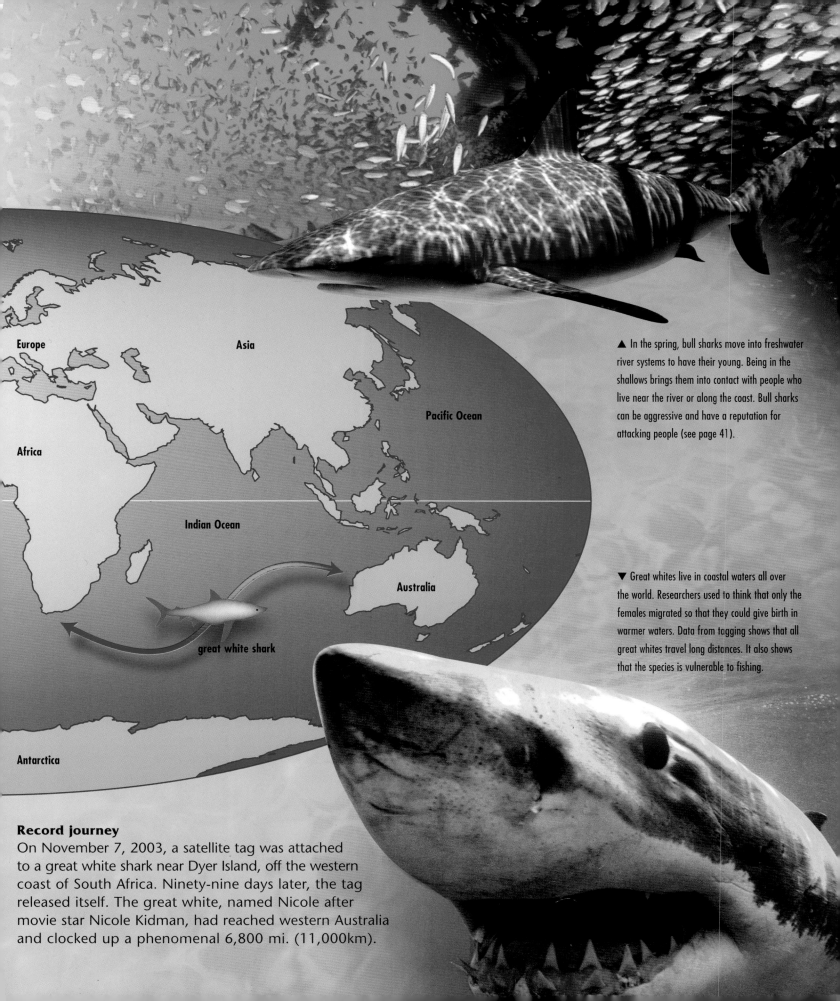

Europe

Asia

Africa

Pacific Ocean

Indian Ocean

Australia

great white shark

Antarctica

▲ In the spring, bull sharks move into freshwater river systems to have their young. Being in the shallows brings them into contact with people who live near the river or along the coast. Bull sharks can be aggressive and have a reputation for attacking people (see page 41).

▼ Great whites live in coastal waters all over the world. Researchers used to think that only the females migrated so that they could give birth in warmer waters. Data from tagging shows that all great whites travel long distances. It also shows that the species is vulnerable to fishing.

Record journey
On November 7, 2003, a satellite tag was attached to a great white shark near Dyer Island, off the western coast of South Africa. Ninety-nine days later, the tag released itself. The great white, named Nicole after movie star Nicole Kidman, had reached western Australia and clocked up a phenomenal 6,800 mi. (11,000km).

Open ocean

The ocean expanses are home to many different pelagic (open-water) sharks. The larger sharks swim close to or at the surface. There are vast distances to cover, and in open water, they need speed to catch fast-moving fish prey such as tuna, mackerel, and marlins. Occasionally, both the great white and the shortfin mako have been known to breach, or leap up out of the water, while hunting.

Hunting the seas

To be an efficient open-ocean hunter, a shark must be either large and powerful or exceptionally streamlined. Large oceanic sharks include the oceanic whitetip, silky, blue, and thresher sharks. They spend most of their time cruising slowly at the surface but are capable of a rapid burst of speed in pursuit of prey. The most streamlined oceanic sharks include the torpedo-shaped porbeagle and salmon sharks, as well as the shortfin mako, which is the fastest shark of all.

▲ Blue sharks, found in tropical and temperate oceans worldwide, are the most common of the large pelagic sharks. They measure around 11.5 ft. (3.5m) long and are easily recognized by their deep blue backs and sides. These blue sharks are hunting anchovies in the Pacific Ocean.

◄ At 10 ft. (3m) long, the pelagic thresher is the smallest and least known of the three species of thresher sharks that live in the open ocean. Its scythelike tail—an extended caudal fin—is around the same length as its body. The shark may use it as a weapon to slash or stun fish or possibly even to herd them.

Supercharged predators

Most sharks are ectothermic (cold-blooded), which means that they take on the temperatures of their surroundings. However, some of the faster-moving oceanic sharks are partly endothermic (warm-blooded), which means that they are able to increase their body temperatures. The common thresher shark can maintain a body temperature as much as 55°F (13°C) higher than the surrounding water. Scientists believe that, by warming parts of their bodies, such as their flanks, these sharks are able to beat their tails more—and pursue their prey more quickly.

▶ Oceanic whitetip sharks are fierce, solitary predators. They live in open water, usually at depths of almost 500 ft. (150m), and are only occasionally seen close to land. They eat a wide variety of food, including turtles, sea birds, and tuna (which they catch by swimming through tuna schools with their mouths open).

Deep-sea hunters

Sharks are successful even in the cold, dark depths of the oceans. Some, such as the Greenland shark, are slow moving and cold-blooded, having the same temperature as the very cold water in which they swim. Others, such as the Galápagos shark, are fast-moving visitors to these dark regions. A few make their own eerie light to lure prey in the gloom.

▲ *Alvin* was the first deep-sea submersible to be able to carry passengers. It has been in operation since 1964. It can dive to a maximum depth of 14,760 ft. (4,500m) and has enabled scientists to observe deep-sea sharks in their habitat.

Down in the depths
Sharks that live deep below the surface are usually small. They often have blunt noses that they use to forage for food and tails that are flat or have large upper lobes. They swim sluggishly because the cold slows down their metabolism (how their body makes energy from food). And they usually give birth to only two or three young at one time.

Gonatus squid

cookie-cutter shark

▲ The cookie-cutter shark, found at depths of 280–11,500 ft. (85–3,500m), has a cigar-shaped body up to 19.5 in. (50cm) long. Around its middle it has a network of photophores— round, light-producing organs that give off a greenish glow. Its light brings curious prey within reach of the shark's wickedly sharp teeth.

great lanternshark

▲ The great lanternshark has been found at depths of 14,760 ft. (4,500m). In deeper waters, more females are found than males. The sharks, up to 25 in. (65cm) long, also get smaller as the depth increases. Lanternsharks are named for their light-producing photophores, which attract prey such as deep-sea squids and crustaceans.

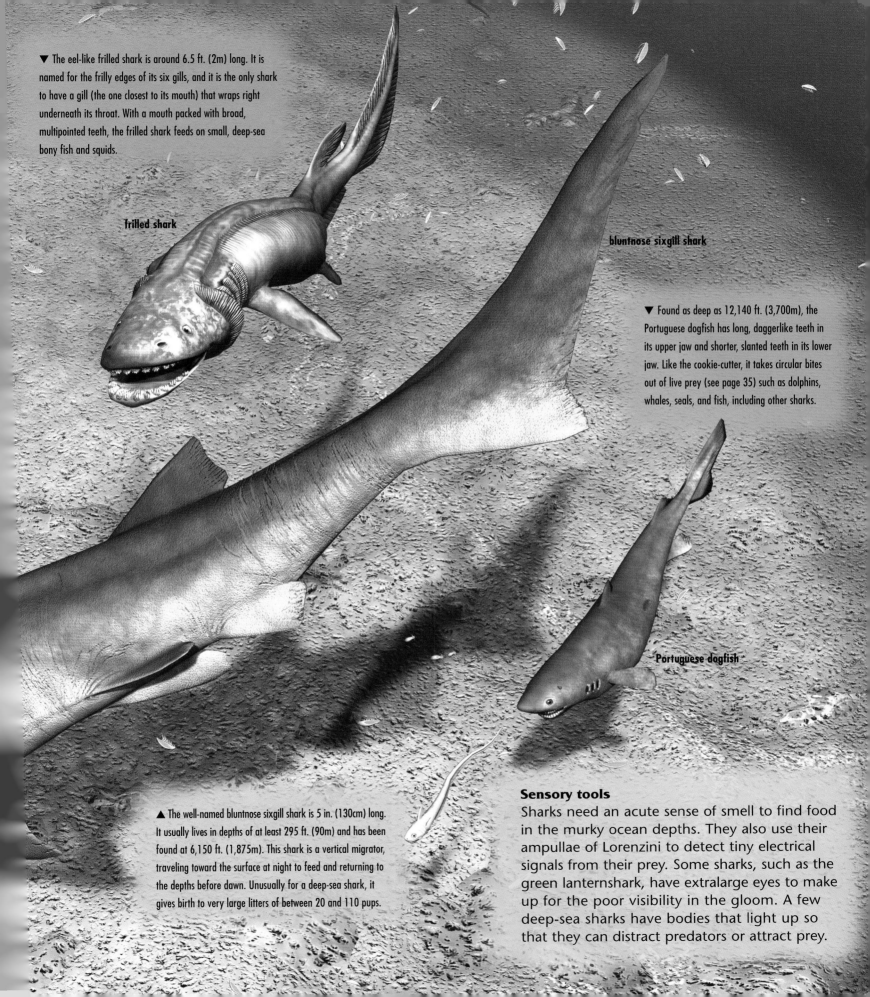

▼ The eel-like frilled shark is around 6.5 ft. (2m) long. It is named for the frilly edges of its six gills, and it is the only shark to have a gill (the one closest to its mouth) that wraps right underneath its throat. With a mouth packed with broad, multipointed teeth, the frilled shark feeds on small, deep-sea bony fish and squids.

frilled shark

bluntnose sixgill shark

▼ Found as deep as 12,140 ft. (3,700m), the Portuguese dogfish has long, daggerlike teeth in its upper jaw and shorter, slanted teeth in its lower jaw. Like the cookie-cutter, it takes circular bites out of live prey (see page 35) such as dolphins, whales, seals, and fish, including other sharks.

Portuguese dogfish

▲ The well-named bluntnose sixgill shark is 5 in. (130cm) long. It usually lives in depths of at least 295 ft. (90m) and has been found at 6,150 ft. (1,875m). This shark is a vertical migrator, traveling toward the surface at night to feed and returning to the depths before dawn. Unusually for a deep-sea shark, it gives birth to very large litters of between 20 and 110 pups.

Sensory tools
Sharks need an acute sense of smell to find food in the murky ocean depths. They also use their ampullae of Lorenzini to detect tiny electrical signals from their prey. Some sharks, such as the green lanternshark, have extralarge eyes to make up for the poor visibility in the gloom. A few deep-sea sharks have bodies that light up so that they can distract predators or attract prey.

On a reef

The clear waters surrounding coral reefs are home to many types of sharks. In the Bahamas, lemon sharks give birth in shallow bays surrounded by mangroves. Galápagos sharks swim in schools off tropical islands around the world, and sand tiger sharks hover above the bottom of rocky reefs off South Africa. Coral reefs provide a rich habitat because they shelter turtles, fish, anemones, crustaceans, and mollusks for sharks to hunt.

▶ With its downturned mouth and the ridges above its eyes, the whitetip reef shark can appear to be frowning. It is named for the distinctive tips on its dorsal and upper caudal fins. It locates prey, such as octopuses and crabs, by sounds and vibrations, traps them in rocky crevices, and then wiggles its slender body in after them.

▼ The epaulette carpet shark is easily identified by the ocellus (a large black eyelike spot) just above each pectoral fin. It is a bottom dweller that uses its pectoral fins to "walk" or even "run" along the seabed. Only 3 ft. (1m) long, it hunts at night for crabs, shrimp, and small fish hiding among the coral.

Balancing act

The three most common sharks in Indo-Pacific coral reefs are the whitetip reef, blacktip reef, and gray reef sharks. Although they are interested in similar prey, they do not have to compete with one another. They either hunt at different times of the day or at the same times but at different depths. The whitetip reef shark is a night hunter that seeks out prey in waters 30–130 ft. (10–40m) deep. The other two species both hunt at dawn and dusk. However, the blacktip pursues prey in lagoons close to the shore, while the gray reef feeds farther out in clearer waters up to 300 ft. (100m) deep.

The world's largest reef

At least 120 species of sharks and rays can be found in the Great Barrier Reef off northern Australia. They range from the epaulette carpet shark that never moves off the reef to migratory species such as the whale shark. Some of the sharks, including whitetip reef sharks, have thick skin to protect against the sharp corals. The colorful fish and shellfish attract bottom feeders such as angel sharks and zebra bullheads, as well as fast hunters such as tiger sharks. Sometimes the tables are turned when large coral grouper fish prey upon the smaller reef sharks.

► Gray reef sharks are active and social sharks that patrol a reef for squids and fish, sometimes in large schools of up to 100 individuals. They measure around 5 ft. (1.6m) long and are prey to larger sharks, including the silvertip shark.

▼ With its spotted body, the zebra shark appears to have been given the wrong name, but it is named for its brown-and-cream striped young. Like many species that swim in bright, shallow waters, zebra sharks have tiny eyes. They hunt at night for mollusks, small fish, and even sea snakes.

SUMMARY OF CHAPTER 1: MEET THE SHARK

Rulers of the oceans

The world of the shark is a complex one. The 375 species in the shark family are very different in appearance and lifestyle. However, what they do have in common—their physical characteristics and their abilities as predatory hunters—has helped them survive successfully for millions of years. During all this time, they have maintained their position as the main predators in the marine food chain.

Classifying the shark

All biologists classify living things according to the system known as Linnaeus, devised by Carolus Linnaeus. He was a Swedish naturalist who published his *Systema Naturae* in 1758. Under his system, which was based on observing external characteristics, shark classification is relatively straightforward. Today, however, the classification system is being modified all the time as more and more is discovered about particular species of sharks.

A variety of habitats

Sharks live in pelagic (open-ocean) and benthic (bottom-dwelling) habitats worldwide. The pelagic sharks are sleek and streamlined and clearly designed for speed. They include the fastest sharks such as the mako shark, with its sprint speed of more than 20 body lengths per second. Benthic sharks look very different—most have blunt noses and many have flat bodies. They swim slowly and often ambush, rather than chase, their prey. Some, such as the angel shark, are very well camouflaged.

The puffadder shyshark is hard to spot in its reef habitat off the coast of South Africa.

Go further . . .

Find out about the biology of sharks and rays: www.elasmo-research.org

Discover exactly how sharks work: www.science.howstuffworks.com/shark6

Investigate this great site that covers all aspects of sharks and rays: www.seaworld.org/animal-info/info-books/sharks-&-rays/

The Florida Museum of Natural History web site recommends books and advises about how to avoid a shark attack: www.flmnh.ufl.edu/fish/Kids/kids.htm

Eyewitness: Shark by Miranda MacQuitty (DK Children, 2000)

Ichthyologist
A zoologist who specializes in fish.

Naturalist
A person who studies or is an expert in natural history.

Paleontologist
A scientist who studies the forms of life that existed in prehistoric times.

Scientist
An expert in at least one area of science who uses scientific methods to conduct research.

Zoologist
A scientist who studies animals and their characteristics and classifies them.

Visit all types of sharks, sawfish, and rays at North America's only predator-based aquarium:
Shark Reef, Mandalay Bay Resort
3950 Las Vegas Blvd.
South Las Vegas, NV 89119
Phone: (702) 632-7777

See shark exhibits at: Natural History Museum Cromwell Road
London SW7 5BD, U.K.
Phone: +44 (0)20 7942 5000
www.nhm.ac.uk

Attend "shark week" each August at:
The Aquarium of Niagara
701 Whirlpool Street
Niagara Falls, NY 14301
Phone: (716) 285-3575
www.aquariumofniagara.org

Shark attack!

Although they are the fiercest of predators, sharks do not naturally feed on humans. Fewer than a dozen of the 375 species of sharks are really considered dangerous to people—and their attacks may be cases of mistaken identities. Sharks could confuse the shape of a human, especially on a surfboard, with a seal or a sea lion. In other instances, they may be provoked by boats that are too close to their food source or pups. Sharks are the ocean's main predators, and most have no need to fear attacks from other hunters. Only a few smaller ones are attacked—by other sharks or by killer whales. When the fiercest shark of all, the great white, hunts, it may kill its prey with a burst of speed that throws the animal right out of the water. It probably does this to stun the animal and avoid being injured by claws or teeth.

A great white shark breaches with a Cape fur seal in its jaws.

Teeth

Sharks' jaws carry an incredible conveyor belt of teeth that are perfectly designed to catch and eat prey. Every time a tooth, or row of teeth, falls out, the conveyor belt carries new teeth forward. The process continues endlessly until the animal dies. Some of the biggest sharks, such as the whale shark, have the smallest teeth. Instead of chewing their food, they filter it using their gill rakers (see pages 42–43).

▶ A gray nurse shark goes in for the kill. Its lower jaw has dropped down, and the upper jaw has moved forward to expose the top teeth. Moments before it makes contact, nictitating membranes (inner eyelids) close to protect its eyes against scratches from the struggling prey.

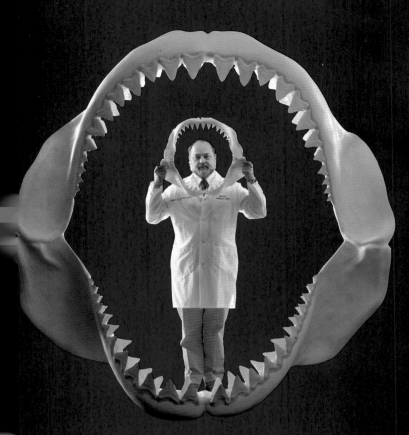

▲ A scientist who specializes in fossil reconstruction stands inside a lifesize model of the prehistoric shark *Megalodon*'s jaws, which are estimated to have been 7 ft. (2.1m) tall and 6 ft. (1.8m) wide. He is holding the actual jaws of a large great white shark. *Megalodon*'s jaw size is estimated from the size of fossil teeth.

Teeth through the ages

Like sharks themselves, sharks' teeth have become smaller since prehistoric times. However, their effectiveness has not diminished. The extinct giant shark *Megalodon* (see page 14), which hunted enormous whales, had serrated teeth that were up to 6 in. (15cm) long—the size of a person's hand. Its modern relative, the great white shark, may be half the size, but it is also the main predator in its habitat. It uses its 3-in. (7.5-cm)-long teeth to bite and weaken its prey.

▼ The cookie-cutter shark got its name because it takes cookie-shaped bites out of larger marine animals such as dolphins and whales. It attaches its lips to its victim by suction and then spins its eel-like body. The small, upright teeth in its upper jaw and the large, triangular teeth in its lower jaw cut out a piece of flesh.

Teeth for every occasion

The slender, spearlike teeth in the jaws of gray nurse, lemon, and shortfin mako sharks are used to catch slippery fish and squids. Bullhead, nurse, and smoothhound sharks are equipped with blunt, crushing teeth for tackling the tough shells of mollusks or crustaceans. Both fearsome great white sharks and tiger sharks have triangular cutting teeth, perfect for taking chunks out of seals and other large prey.

▲ The swellshark is a nocturnal hunter that lives in kelp forests in the eastern Pacific Ocean, from California to central Chile. It is 3 ft. (1m) long and has a large mouth filled with rows of tiny, pointed teeth. They are very sharp and used to grab hold of the fish and crustaceans that the swellshark catches on or close to the seabed.

Targeting prey

Sharks have five senses, just like humans: sight, hearing, touch, smell, and taste. They also use pressure sensors along their bodies to detect the movement of prey as far as 30 ft. (10m) away. And sharks have another remarkable sense—electrosensory perception. This allows them to detect the weak electrical field generated by all marine animals.

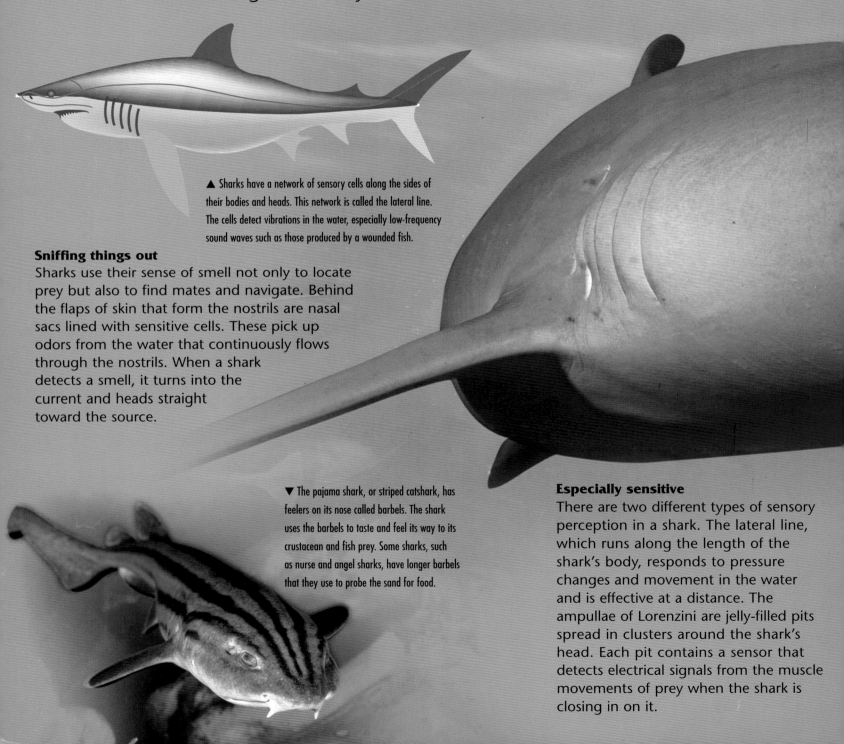

▼ The Caribbean reef shark patrols coral reefs from Florida to Brazil, but it is especially common in the Caribbean Sea. Its main prey is large fish such as tuna. The Caribbean reef shark is very sensitive to the very low-frequency sounds that travel through water, and this enables it to target moving fish easily.

▲ Sharks have a network of sensory cells along the sides of their bodies and heads. This network is called the lateral line. The cells detect vibrations in the water, especially low-frequency sound waves such as those produced by a wounded fish.

Sniffing things out

Sharks use their sense of smell not only to locate prey but also to find mates and navigate. Behind the flaps of skin that form the nostrils are nasal sacs lined with sensitive cells. These pick up odors from the water that continuously flows through the nostrils. When a shark detects a smell, it turns into the current and heads straight toward the source.

▼ The pajama shark, or striped catshark, has feelers on its nose called barbels. The shark uses the barbels to taste and feel its way to its crustacean and fish prey. Some sharks, such as nurse and angel sharks, have longer barbels that they use to probe the sand for food.

Especially sensitive

There are two different types of sensory perception in a shark. The lateral line, which runs along the length of the shark's body, responds to pressure changes and movement in the water and is effective at a distance. The ampullae of Lorenzini are jelly-filled pits spread in clusters around the shark's head. Each pit contains a sensor that detects electrical signals from the muscle movements of prey when the shark is closing in on it.

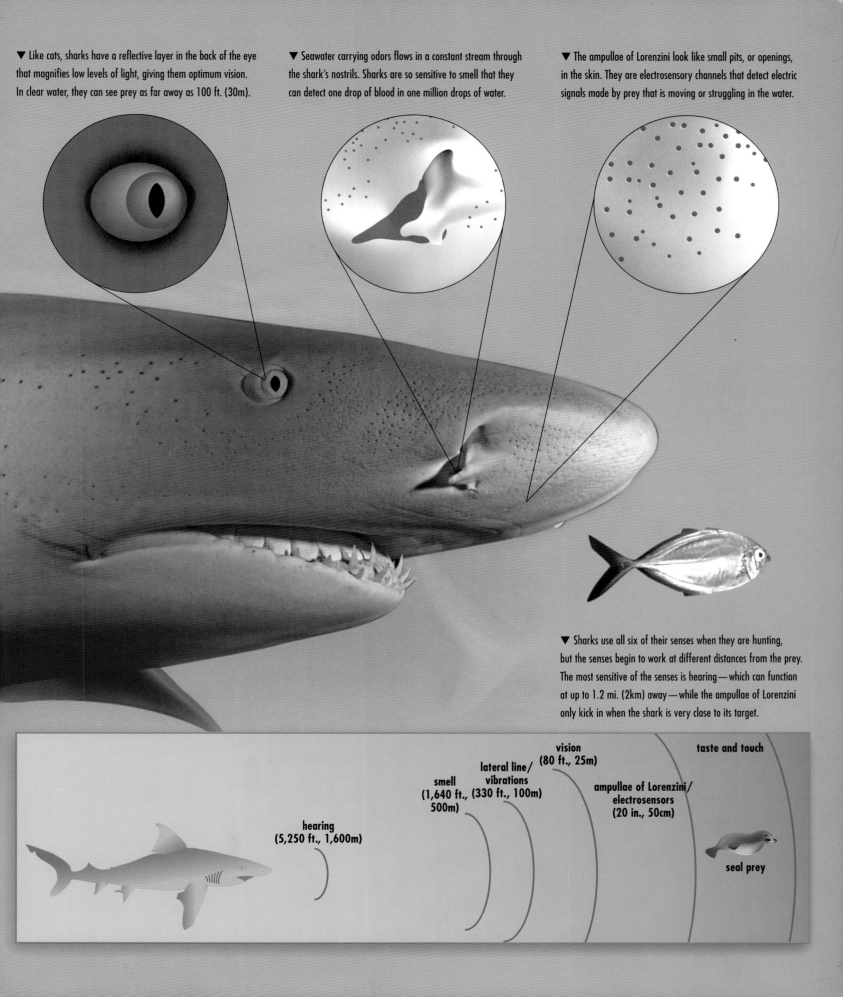

▼ Like cats, sharks have a reflective layer in the back of the eye that magnifies low levels of light, giving them optimum vision. In clear water, they can see prey as far away as 100 ft. (30m).

▼ Seawater carrying odors flows in a constant stream through the shark's nostrils. Sharks are so sensitive to smell that they can detect one drop of blood in one million drops of water.

▼ The ampullae of Lorenzini look like small pits, or openings, in the skin. They are electrosensory channels that detect electric signals made by prey that is moving or struggling in the water.

▼ Sharks use all six of their senses when they are hunting, but the senses begin to work at different distances from the prey. The most sensitive of the senses is hearing — which can function at up to 1.2 mi. (2km) away — while the ampullae of Lorenzini only kick in when the shark is very close to its target.

vision
(80 ft., 25m)

taste and touch

lateral line/
vibrations
(330 ft., 100m)

smell
(1,640 ft.,
500m)

ampullae of Lorenzini/
electrosensors
(20 in., 50cm)

hearing
(5,250 ft., 1,600m)

seal prey

Hunting in packs

Not all sharks are lone killers. Blue sharks are one of many species that feed in groups, while gray nurse and copper sharks cooperate to hunt prey. These sharks have developed such techniques because they allow them to catch more food than they could by hunting on their own.

▶ These copper sharks in the Indian Ocean have created a huge bait ball of sardines. As they charge through the bait ball, they snatch big mouthfuls of the fish. Sometimes dolphins join sharks to prey on large bait balls like this one.

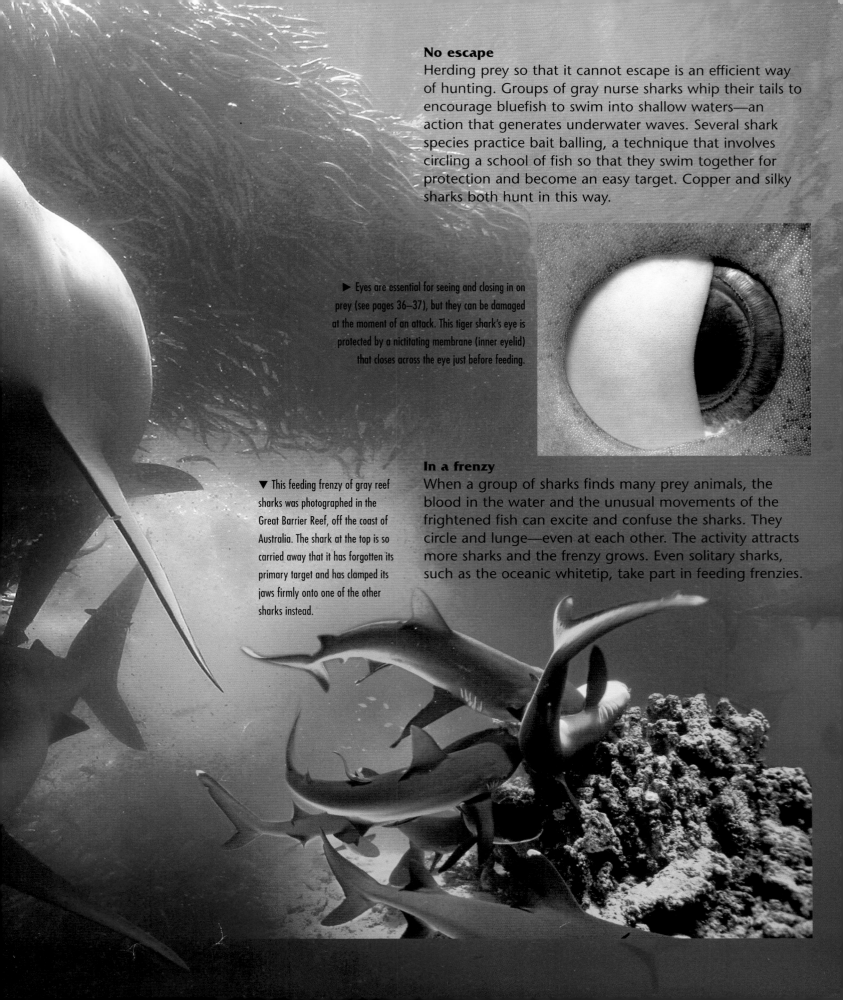

No escape

Herding prey so that it cannot escape is an efficient way of hunting. Groups of gray nurse sharks whip their tails to encourage bluefish to swim into shallow waters—an action that generates underwater waves. Several shark species practice bait balling, a technique that involves circling a school of fish so that they swim together for protection and become an easy target. Copper and silky sharks both hunt in this way.

▶ Eyes are essential for seeing and closing in on prey (see pages 36–37), but they can be damaged at the moment of an attack. This tiger shark's eye is protected by a nictitating membrane (inner eyelid) that closes across the eye just before feeding.

▼ This feeding frenzy of gray reef sharks was photographed in the Great Barrier Reef, off the coast of Australia. The shark at the top is so carried away that it has forgotten its primary target and has clamped its jaws firmly onto one of the other sharks instead.

In a frenzy

When a group of sharks finds many prey animals, the blood in the water and the unusual movements of the frightened fish can excite and confuse the sharks. They circle and lunge—even at each other. The activity attracts more sharks and the frenzy grows. Even solitary sharks, such as the oceanic whitetip, take part in feeding frenzies.

Man-eaters

According to the International Shark Attack File (ISAF), which reports on shark attacks worldwide, three sharks pose the greatest threat to people: great white, tiger, and bull sharks. However, the total number of shark attack victims is fewer than 100 per year, of which only 5–15 are fatal. A person is 250 times more likely to be killed by lightning than by a shark.

▼ The great white shark often attacks by rising up at a steep angle from below the water. It takes a bite and then releases its prey, wounded but alive. The shark circles and waits for the prey to weaken from blood loss before returning to kill and feed. This bite-spit-wait technique is very effective.

▲ Although there are very few shark attacks, they are still terrible. Beaches post warning signs in areas where they are likely to happen. This sign alerts swimmers, surfers, and divers to danger from some of the 40 species of sharks in Hawaiian waters.

Most feared

The great white shark has the worst reputation of the man-eaters and carries out more fatal attacks each year than any other shark. With triangular, razor-sharp teeth up to 3 in. (7.5cm) long and the ability to smell a drop of blood in more than 100 qt. (100L) of water, it is a truly frightening predator. It is difficult to be exact about shark attack statistics because it is not always certain which species of sharks carried out which attacks. However, the International Shark Attack File estimates that there have been only 430 attacks by great whites since 1580.

Other killers

The tiger shark is a large, aggressive shark that swims in tropical oceans. It is 10 ft. (3m) long and a voracious hunter. Its diet is very varied, and it is notorious for its attacks on divers and surfers. The bull shark is also very feared. It is a marine shark, but it can tolerate fresh water and often travels up rivers. It has been responsible for many attacks on bathers and swimmers in the Ganges, Zambezi, and Amazon rivers.

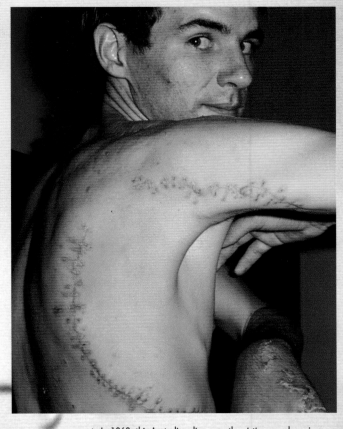

▲ In 1963, this Australian diver was the victim—and survivor—of one of the best documented near-fatal encounters with a great white shark. Rodney Fox, who was taking part in a spearfishing competition, suffered three attacks before he escaped by grabbing the shark's snout. His wounds needed 462 stitches. Today, Fox campaigns for the conservation of great white sharks.

Giant filter feeders

The filter feeders of the shark world are enormous. This is because they often travel a long way to find the zooplankton on which they feed—whale sharks will follow plankton blooms all over the eastern Indian Ocean. Filter feeders need a large storage capacity and a large mouth so that when they do find food, they can process huge quantities of it.

▶ This sample of zooplankton, photographed under a microscope, is from the Great Barrier Reef in Australia. It includes the larvae of sea cucumbers, copepods (small crustaceans), and crabs. Zooplankton is seasonal—more food is available during the spring and summer months than during the winter.

▼ The 30-ft. (10-m)-long basking shark cruises close to the surface at 2.5 mph (4km/h) with its cavernous jaws stretched wide, revealing its white gill arches and the bristly black gill rakers in between. At regular intervals, the shark closes its mouth, flutters its gills, and swallows the plankton that it has collected.

Ways of feeding

Only three living sharks are filter feeders: the whale shark, basking shark, and megamouth. These sharks all forage in the same way. They swim forward with open mouths, passively scooping up anything in their path. At regular intervals, they close their mouths, water is pushed out through the gills, and prey filtered through the gill rakers is swallowed. This is filter feeding. The whale shark and megamouth also suction feed, actively sucking in prey.

Deep-water monster

The megamouth is more than 16 ft. (5m) long and is named for its gigantic, 3-ft. (1-m)-wide mouth. It has up to 100 rows of tiny teeth in each jaw and an enormous tongue. It also has bioluminescent spots called photophores around its mouth that may attract plankton and small fish.

▶ Whale sharks are often followed by remoras, 3-ft. (1-m)-long fish with suckers on their heads, which they use to attach themselves to their host's stomach. The remoras gain a free ride, protection from predators, and a good place from which to ambush prey. They can also eat any scraps of food that may fall from the shark's mouth.

megamouth filter feeding with mouth open

megamouth suction feeding with jaw extended

▲ When the megamouth suction feeds, it juts out its upper jaw and widens its throat. By doing this, it creates a suction that pulls in seawater that is filled with zooplankton. Then it closes its mouth and the food is filtered in the usual way by the gill rakers.

Bottom feeders

The seabed is rich in pickings for sharks that have adapted to living there. These benthos, or bottom feeders, live on or close to the seabed. Some have flattened bodies and markings or colors that help them hide from and ambush passing prey or protect them from larger predators. Some crawl along the bottom on their fins, searching for prey in the sand, mud, or seaweed. Others glide around coral reefs and rocky areas, sucking out food from rocks and crevices.

▼ The tasseled wobbegong lives in the warm seas of the western Pacific Ocean. It is well camouflaged against the rocks and coral reefs. Its shaggy beard of tentacles looks like seaweed and attracts prey including flatfish, squids, cuttlefish, and crabs.

The angel shark lies flat on the seabed.

The pectoral fins flip sand over the body.

Eventually only the eyes will be visible.

▲ Small groups of tawny nurse sharks up to 10 ft. (3m) long rest in a heap under reef overhangs during the day. They split up at night to forage for food, using the barbels on their noses to seek out shrimp, sea urchins, crabs, octopuses, and squids. Their throats act like powerful pumps to suck up the prey.

Life on the seabed

Sharks that live on or close to the bottom of the ocean are usually slow moving. They rely on camouflage for protection and have jaws that are adapted for feeding from the seabed. Although most sharks do not sleep and need to keep swimming in order to breathe, some of these bottom feeders, including nurse, smoothhound, and leopard sharks, rest in groups during the day. They breathe by opening and closing their mouths to push water through the gills.

Surprise attack!

Ambushing becomes easy if the prey cannot detect the presence of the hunter. Intricate colors and patterns hide flat-bodied predators such as angel sharks. The striped catshark and zebra bullhead shark both have a disruptive pattern of stripes that confuses both predators and prey. Epaulette and necklace carpet sharks have spotted skin that help them "disappear" in the dappled waters.

▲ Angel sharks are up to 6.5 ft. (2m) long. They bury themselves in the sand or mud and then burst out to grasp prey in their viselike jaws. They travel up to 2.5 mi. (4km) each night from ambush site to ambush site, hunting fish, skates, crustaceans, and mollusks.

SUMMARY OF CHAPTER 2: SHARK ATTACK!

Perfect predators

Sharks are superb at hunting, and they are also efficient killers. Most sharks use their sharp teeth to catch prey, but the largest ones, such as the whale and basking sharks, are filter feeders. Some sharks hunt cooperatively, working together in groups or herding fish with their tails. All animals use their senses to target prey, but sharks' senses are especially acute. Sharks have the added advantages of being able to detect the movements of prey using their lateral line system. They also detect the electric fields around prey using their electrosensory ampullae of Lorenzini.

The truth about sharks

Sharks are not bloodthirsty killers: they hunt to survive. By preying upon animals that are lower down the food chain, sharks help keep the oceans' ecosystems in balance. The reality about shark attacks on people is that there are very few per year—only around 50–70 worldwide, of which between 5–15 are fatal. It is difficult to give accurate shark attack statistics because eyewitnesses may have trouble identifying the species, while some attacks are simply not witnessed or reported.

The ISAF

The International Shark Attack File (ISAF) is an organization that compiles the world's most accurate list of shark attacks. It is managed by the American Elasmobranch Society and the Florida Museum of Natural History. The information collected for the ISAF dates as far back as the mid-1500s, and the data has been submitted and investigated by scientists all over the world.

This close-up shows the curved teeth of a blue shark. The hooked shape and serrated edges enable the shark to hold onto slippery squids and fish.

Go further . . .

Shark attacks throughout the ages and throughout the world are detailed here: www.shark-info.com/shark-history

For up-to-the-minute statistics on shark attacks worldwide, visit: www.sharkattackfile.net

To learn how to avoid a shark attack, consult the International Shark Attack File at: www.flmnh.ufl.edu/fish/kids/Avoid/avoid.htm

The Encyclopedia of Sharks by Steve and Jane Parker (Firefly Books, 2005)

The Truth About Great White Sharks by Mary M. Cerullo and Jeffrey L. Rotman (Chronicle Books, 2006)

Diver
A person who dives or works underwater, often using a breathing apparatus and weighted clothing.

Microbiologist
A biologist who specializes in microorganisms and their structure.

Oceanographer
A scientist who explores and studies all aspects of the oceans, including their physical geography and the animals and plants that live in them.

Statistician
A mathematician who gathers data and studies and compares it.

The San Diego Natural History Museum has an online "Shark School," or visit to find out about sharks, including ten local species:
San Diego Natural History Museum
1788 El Prado
San Diego, CA 92101
Phone: (619) 232-3821
www.sdnhm.org

Visit New England Aquarium's four-story underwater home to hundreds of fish, including sharks, sea turtles, and barracudas (also see it online at: www.earthcam.com/network):
New England Aquarium
Central Wharf
Boston, MA 02110
Phone: (617) 973-5200
www.neaq.org

CHAPTER 3

Sharks and people

It is slowly dawning on people that sharks do not pose as great of a threat as they had feared, but there is still a long way to go. By 2017, an estimated 20 species of living sharks will have become extinct. Sharks are still ruthlessly hunted for food, trophies, skins, and traditional medicines. Thousands more are trapped each year in nets that were either intended to catch other fish or set up to keep sharks away from beaches. Pollution poisons the whole food chain and threatens shark nurseries. Many species grow slowly, mate late, and produce relatively few offspring. These species are in real danger of being killed before they have had a chance to reproduce. Sharks help keep populations of prey animals in check. By fishing too many sharks or putting them in danger in other ways, people put entire ecosystems at risk. It is essential that all countries help monitor and preserve shark populations.

From the safety of a shark cage, divers watch Galápagos sharks off the coast of Hawaii.

Myths and legends

Sharks are sea monsters in mythology; gods or demons in traditional cultures; and the subject of paintings, sculptures, and stories all over the world. Shark legends have been around since prehistoric times, but the first written accounts of sharks are from the ancient Greeks, who believed that sharks were a source of magical powers.

Around the world

Mythical sharks appear in many guises. In Japan, the storm god Samehito is known as the "shark man," while the Hawaiians had a shark god named Moho. Some peoples build myths around the actions of sharks. The Warao Indians of the Orinoco River basin in South America tell of Nohi-Abassi, a man who trained a shark to kill his mother-in-law but was killed himself, his leg becoming the constellation Orion. In the South Pacific, people on the Solomon Islands believed that sharks were their ancestors and offered them human sacrifices.

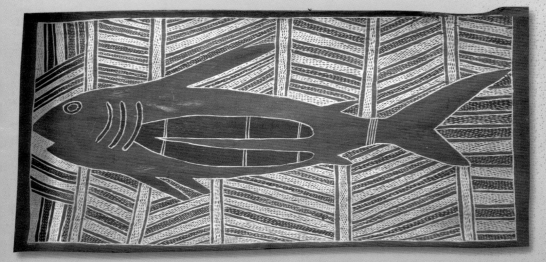

▲ In the art of the Aboriginal people of Australia, the shark represents an ancestral spirit. This bark painting of a tiger shark is part of the x-ray tradition, a 4,000-year-old painting style that shows an animal's internal organs and bone structure.

▶ Jonah disappears inside the mouth of a big fish in an illustration from a Hebrew manuscript of 1299. The 16th-century French naturalist Guillaume Rondelet suggested that the Biblical story was wrong and that Jonah was swallowed by a shark, not a whale.

▲ These American A-10 aircraft, or Flying Tigers, are painted
to resemble tiger sharks. The practice was started by Chinese
fighter pilots, who decorated their planes as sharks in order
to terrify their Japanese enemies. In Japanese mythology,
the shark is associated with the demon storm god.

The shark charmers

Being able to control or charm sharks has been an
important part of life for several cultures. In 1298, the
Italian explorer Marco Polo recorded a visit to Ceylon
(present-day Sri Lanka) where pearl fishermen refused to
dive unless protected by a magic spell or charm. The Fiji
islanders also relied on shark charmers who carried out
a shark-kissing ceremony twice each year in order to
protect all of the island's fishing boats from attacks.

▶ The Tlingit tribe of Alaska has a rich ancestral
tradition. Each person belongs to a clan associated
with an animal. This shark mask would have
been worn by one of the Shark clan at
the beginning of the 1900s.

Shark tales

Over the years, sharks have made their appearances in paintings and sculptures, and in more recent times played their part in novels and movies. But it is the man-eaters—the great white and the tiger shark—that obsess people, and the fear of those teeth is exploited by artists, writers, and movie directors.

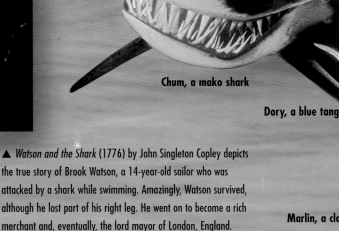

Anchor, a winghead hammerhead

Chum, a mako shark

Dory, a blue tang

Marlin, a clown fish

Sharks in fiction
Most sharks in literature appear during shipwrecks or epic sea battles. In *Moby Dick* (1851), sharks in a feeding frenzy attack the dead sperm whale that Captain Ahab is towing to land. Ernest Hemingway's *The Old Man and the Sea* (1952) tells of mako sharks devouring the marlin that the Old Man has battled for so long to catch.

Sharks in movies
Jaws (1975) was not the first shark movie, but it had a huge impact. It spawned a host of shark horror films, including three more *Jaws* movies, *Deep Blue Sea* (1999), *Open Water* (2004), and the *Shark Attack* films. It also inspired animations such as *Finding Nemo* (2003) and *A Shark's Tale* (2004).

▲ *Watson and the Shark* (1776) by John Singleton Copley depicts the true story of Brook Watson, a 14-year-old sailor who was attacked by a shark while swimming. Amazingly, Watson survived, although he lost part of his right leg. He went on to become a rich merchant and, eventually, the lord mayor of London, England.

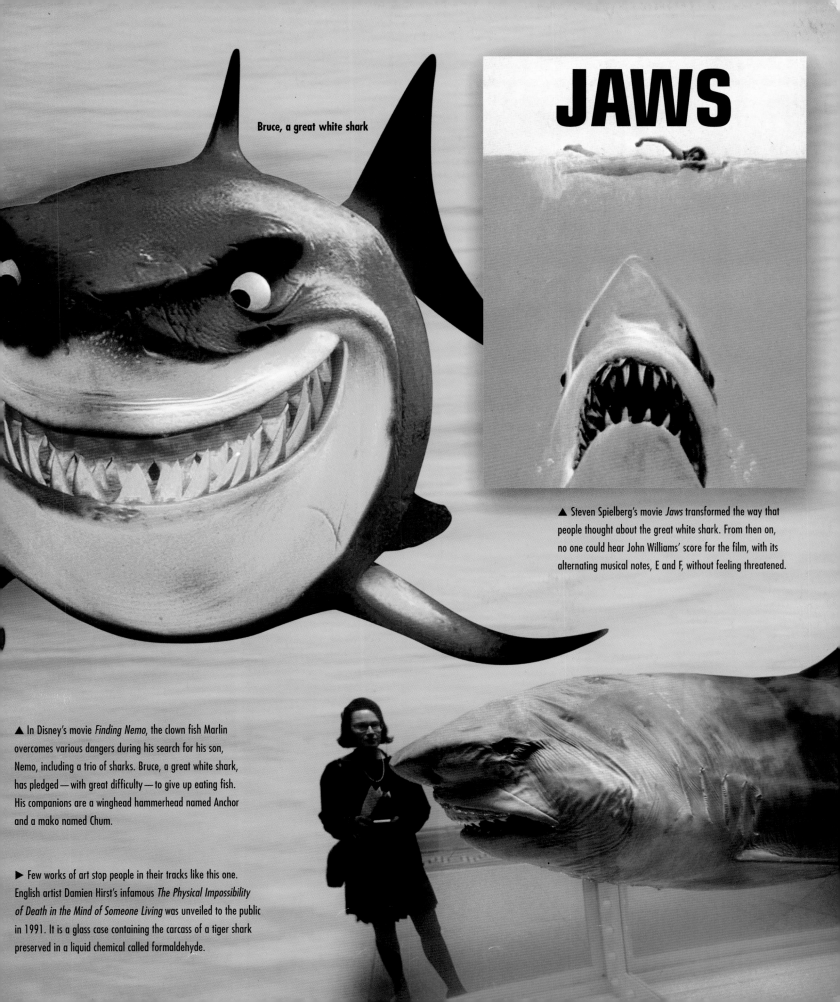

Bruce, a great white shark

JAWS

▲ Steven Spielberg's movie *Jaws* transformed the way that people thought about the great white shark. From then on, no one could hear John Williams' score for the film, with its alternating musical notes, E and F, without feeling threatened.

▲ In Disney's movie *Finding Nemo*, the clown fish Marlin overcomes various dangers during his search for his son, Nemo, including a trio of sharks. Bruce, a great white shark, has pledged — with great difficulty — to give up eating fish. His companions are a winghead hammerhead named Anchor and a mako named Chum.

▶ Few works of art stop people in their tracks like this one. English artist Damien Hirst's infamous *The Physical Impossibility of Death in the Mind of Someone Living* was unveiled to the public in 1991. It is a glass case containing the carcass of a tiger shark preserved in a liquid chemical called formaldehyde.

▼ This newborn Galápagos shark has been snared close to shore in an illegal gill net. The nets are intended for different prey, but they are so delicate that the sharks do not see them. These sharks need to keep moving to breathe, so once they become entangled, they drown.

Threats to sharks

S harks are under attack! Each year, they kill fewer than 20 people, yet in return up to 100 million sharks and rays are killed. More than 50 of the world's shark species are already recognized as endangered or vulnerable, and another 60 are likely to become so in the near future.

Sharks for sale

People fish sharks for sport and food; they make leather from their skins and medicines from their cartilage; and they harvest squalene oil from their livers. They make their teeth into jewelry and sell the jaws as souvenirs. As well as the sharks that are deliberately fished, there are accidental by-catches—sharks caught in nets intended for other fish. However, by far the largest number of deaths are because of finning—cutting off the fins for shark-fin soup.

Habitat destruction

Shark habitats are also under threat. Detergents, pesticides, and other chemicals are flushed into waterways and enter the oceans, where they are absorbed by sharks and their prey. The toxins kill sharks and damage their unborn young. Land development can be another problem. On the Biminis in the Bahamas, for example, the lemon shark's mangrove breeding grounds have been bulldozed to build a resort, causing the survival rate to fall by 30 percent in 11 years.

▲ Shark-fin soup is a delicacy in Japan and China. In Hong Kong, a single dorsal fin from a whale shark or basking shark can bring in the equivalent of around $20,000. Fishermen simply cut off the fin and throw the living shark back into the water to die.

▲ Dead sharks caught by sportfishermen trail behind a boat off the coast of Florida. Sportfishermen hunt sharks for pleasure and collect the jaws as trophies. Sport fishing may reduce the shark population in a small locality, but it is not as serious a threat to sharks as by-catching and finning.

Getting up close

If the threats to sharks are to be reduced, then people need to discover more about the species that they are trying to save. The best way to find out about an animal is to spend time watching it closely in its habitat. Observing the faster and more dangerous sharks has obvious risks, so shark watchers and scientists have devised different ways to protect themselves.

Divers in armor

Ron Taylor is the Australian shark photographer who filmed the live shark sequences for the movie *Jaws*. He came up with the idea of diving in a protective metal mesh suit. In 1979, his wife, fellow shark expert Valerie Taylor, tested one out on gray reef sharks. The suit works with smaller sharks but would offer no protection against a great white shark.

▲ A diver attaches a Shark Shield™ to his leg. This device sends out electronic signals that target the ampullae of Lorenzini (see pages 36–37) around a shark's snout. As the shark approaches the device, the signals become more and more uncomfortable and eventually the shark turns and swims away.

◀ Valerie Taylor successfully tests a lightweight version of the original stainless-steel mesh suit against the bite of a whitetip reef shark off the coast of Australia. This suit has helped the Taylors study in depth how sharks bite and feed.

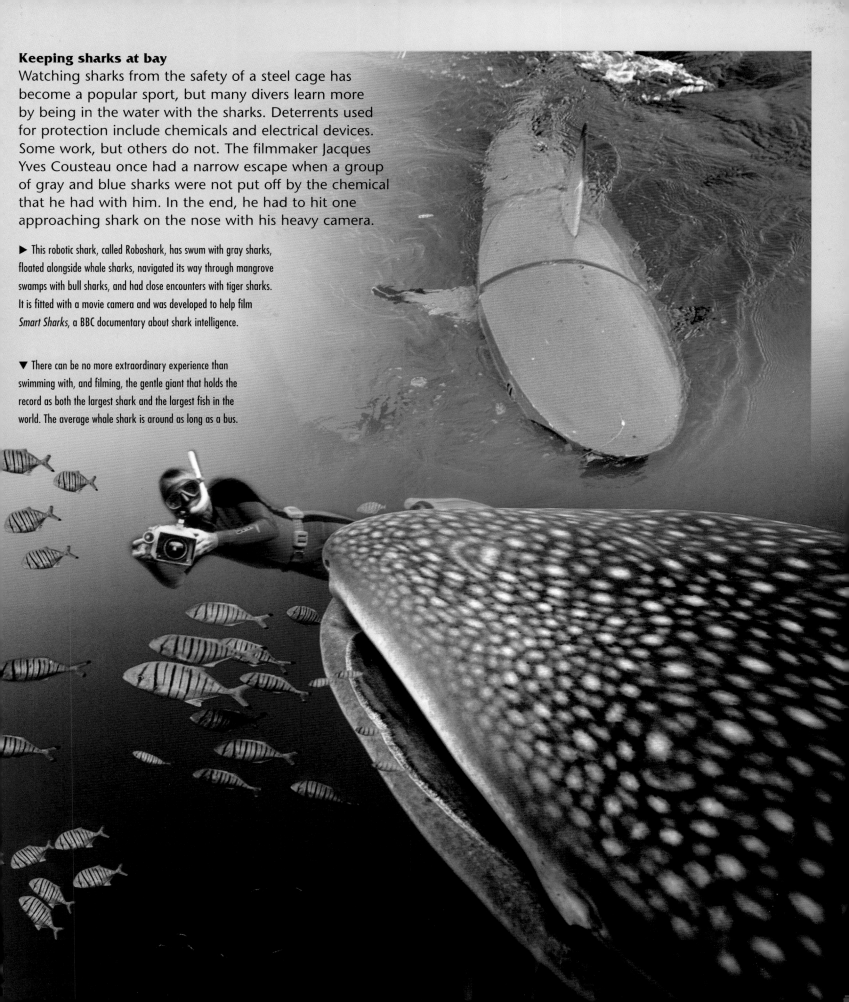

Keeping sharks at bay

Watching sharks from the safety of a steel cage has become a popular sport, but many divers learn more by being in the water with the sharks. Deterrents used for protection include chemicals and electrical devices. Some work, but others do not. The filmmaker Jacques Yves Cousteau once had a narrow escape when a group of gray and blue sharks were not put off by the chemical that he had with him. In the end, he had to hit one approaching shark on the nose with his heavy camera.

▶ This robotic shark, called Roboshark, has swum with gray sharks, floated alongside whale sharks, navigated its way through mangrove swamps with bull sharks, and had close encounters with tiger sharks. It is fitted with a movie camera and was developed to help film *Smart Sharks*, a BBC documentary about shark intelligence.

▼ There can be no more extraordinary experience than swimming with, and filming, the gentle giant that holds the record as both the largest shark and the largest fish in the world. The average whale shark is around as long as a bus.

Conservation

Threatened shark species urgently need help. In the last 15 years alone, numbers of hammerheads and great whites have reduced by 70 percent worldwide. One way to protect sharks is to learn more about them. Scientists and conservationists use accurate research to educate people. They also persuade governments to help, for example by outlawing finning and tackling pollution.

◀ In Kaneohe Bay, Hawaii, marine biologists have been tagging scalloped hammerhead pups. They now know that between 5,000 and 10,000 pups are born in the bay each year. This kind of research helps scientists protect shark habitats.

► This acoustic transmitter has been used to track the movements and behavior of basking sharks in their summer feeding grounds in the Irish Sea. The transmitter sends out pulses of sound that are picked up by a receiver on a research vessel.

Laws to protect sharks

More than 60 countries have banned finning (see page 53), but not all of them have the resources to enforce the law. In 2003, around 300,000 shark fins were exported from Ecuador to China and Hong Kong for shark-fin soup. Then Ecuador banned finning—but the industry is still thriving. The country does not have enough money to police shark fishing effectively.

Taking action

Conservation organizations and marine biologists study sharks in the wild and pass on information about how sharks can be helped. They also try to correct misinformation. For example, many people still believe that sharks are immune to tumors and that squalene from their liver oil can protect people against cancer. By showing that this is a myth, scientists may be able to stop people from killing so many sharks for their oil.

◄ In the Coral Sea off the northeast coast of Australia, two scientists attach a tag to a whitetip reef shark's tail. The tag will record the temperature and depth of the water in which the shark swims and send the data to the scientists' receiving device.

SUMMARY OF CHAPTER 3: SHARKS AND PEOPLE

Sharks through the ages
Throughout human history, sharks have been revered and feared. They have been worshiped as gods, taken center stage in religious ceremonies and rituals, and influenced the actions of many traditional peoples worldwide. They have also played starring roles in movies and books and have made personal appearances in works of art.

Death threat
Many sharks are endangered or under threat of extinction. This is partly because they are hunted and killed by people for food or sport or drowned in nets intended for other fish. Almost 550 species of sharks and rays are thought to be in some sort of danger, more than 100 of which are threatened with extinction. If people do not change their actions—for example, if demand for shark-fin soup continues—this list will only get longer.

Saving the shark
People can change the future of sharks. To begin with, they can find out more about sharks and get contact conservation organizations. They can campaign to stop overfishing and for the reduction in the enormous number of deaths caused through by-catching. They can ban shark-fin soup and avoid shark meat unless it comes from managed fisheries. And they can make sure that any products that they buy, including jewelry, cosmetics, and leather, do not come from sharks.

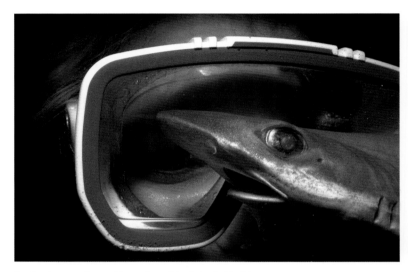

A scientist examines a bigeye houndshark in the Red Sea.

Go further . . .

Discover how you can help protect sharks: www.bbc.co.uk/nature/animals/conservation/sharks/

Make a difference at the Bite-Back site: www.bite-back.com

The Shark Trust gives information about shark education and campaigns: www.sharktrust.org

Animals Under Threat: Great White Shark by Louise and Richard Spilsbury (Heinemann Library, 2004)

Informania: Sharks by Christopher Maynard (Candlewick, 2000)

Conservationist
Someone who works to preserve nature and the environment.

Marine biologist
A scientist who specializes in marine ecology.

Researcher
Someone who studies a subject closely so that he or she can present it in a detailed and accurate way.

Specialist
A scientist who becomes an expert in one subject or part of a subject.

Learn about shark-diving adventures, departing from San Diego, CA, at: Shark Diver
Phone: (415) 404-6144
www.sharkdiver.com

Go basking-shark watching in their summer feeding grounds off the U.K.'s southwestern coast:
Elemental Tours
Cornwall, U.K.
Phone: +44 (0) 1736 811 200
www.elementaltours.co.uk

See sharks in a tropical lagoon habitat at Nausicaa sea life center:
Boulevard Sainte Beuve
62200 Boulogne-sur-Mer, France
Phone: +33 (3) 21 30 98 98
www.nausicaa.fr/Anglais/accveil.htm

Glossary

ampullae (singular: ampulla) of Lorenzini
Jelly-filled pits in the skin of a shark's head that allow it to detect electric signals emitted by other animals.

amulet
A small object worn as a protective charm.

anal fin
A single fin on the stomach between the pelvic and caudal fins of some sharks.

asymmetric
Unbalanced, not of equal length.

bait ball
A ball-shaped mass of fish prey herded together.

barbel
One of two long, whiskerlike lobes on the snouts of some sharks that help locate prey through touch and taste.

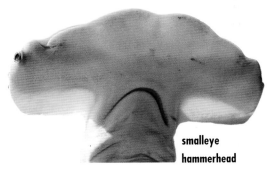
smalleye hammerhead

benthic
Bottom-dwelling.

bioluminescent
Giving out a light produced by living organisms.

bony fish
Any fish with a skeleton made of bone rather than cartilage.

breaching
Leaping out of the water and then splashing back in.

buoyant
Able to float in water. The squalene oil in a shark's liver helps it float, because the oil is much lighter than water.

by-catch
Unwanted fish taken by accident when fishing for a particular species.

camouflage
Markings on the body of an animal that help it blend in with its surroundings.

cartilage
A lightweight, flexible material that makes up the skeleton of a shark.

caudal fin
The fin on the tail of a shark that carries the end of the spinal column.

chimera
A smooth-skinned, cartilaginous fish related to skates and rays.

conservation
Caring for animals, plants, and natural resources so that they do not become extinct or run out.

copepod
A small crustacean often found among zooplankton.

coral
Rock formed from the external skeletons of tiny sea creatures called polyps that pile up to form a reef.

crustacean
An animal without a backbone but with a hard shell and a segmented body. Crabs, shrimp, copepods, and barnacles are all crustaceans.

shark amulet

denticle
A small toothlike scale on the skin of a shark.

dorsal fin
A shark's main fin, located on its back between the head and the caudal fin.

ecology
The scientific study of how living things relate to each other.

ecosystem
A living community of different species that interact.

ectothermic
Cold-blooded, having a body temperature that rises and falls to match the temperature outside.

electrosensory perception
The ability to detect electric signals given off by other animals.

embryo
A developing young animal before it has been born or hatched.

endothermic
Warm-blooded, having a body temperature that stays warm whatever the temperature is outside.

extinct
Describes an animal or plant species that has died out completely.

feeding frenzy
When a group of sharks attack prey and become very aggressive and excited by the blood in the water.

filter feeding
An eating method used by some sharks that involves using the gill rakers to strain plankton and small fish from the water.

finning
Cutting off a shark's fin and then throwing the body back into the water.

food chain
The flow of energy from one living thing to another in a particular environment. Predators such as sharks are at the top of the food chain.

fossil
The preserved remains of an animal or a plant.

gill
An opening on the side or underside of the head of a shark or ray that is used for breathing. Most sharks have five or seven pairs of gills.

gill raker
A comblike part of the gills of some sharks that is used to filter food from the water.

dogfish
egg case

habitat
The environment in which an animal lives.

invertebrate
Having no backbone.

larva (plural: larvae)
A young animal that changes its shape as it grows up.

lateral line
A system of fluid-filled channels that runs from the head along the sides of a shark's body. These detect tiny movements of prey and vibrations in the water.

mammal
An animal with a backbone whose young feed on their mother's milk.

metabolize
To use the metabolism (the physical and chemical systems that keep an animal or plant alive) to change something such as food into energy.

migration
The seasonal movement of animals from one place to another in search of food or a mate or to give birth.

mollusk
An animal without a backbone and with an unsegmented body, usually protected by a hard shell. Mussels, snails, clams, and squids are mollusks.

nictitating membrane
A movable extra eyelid that protects the eyes of some sharks from damage when they attack.

nocturnal
Active at night.

blue shark

ocellus
An eyespot.

oviparous
Describes an animal that lays eggs.

ovoviviparous
Describes an animal that produces eggs that develop and hatch inside the mother's body.

pectoral fin
One of a pair of fins on a shark that are on each side of its body just behind the head.

pelagic
Describes sharks of the open ocean.

pelvic fin
One of a pair of fins on a shark that are on each side of its body between the stomach and tail.

photophore
A small dark spot that can produce light, found on the bodies of some sharks such as lanternsharks.

plankton
Tiny animals and plants, often microscopic, that float near the surface of the ocean.

pollution
Harmful substances and waste that poison the environment.

predator
An animal that hunts and eats other animals.

prey
An animal that is hunted by other, usually larger, animals.

ray
A flat-bodied, cartilaginous fish related to sharks and similar to a skate, except it produces live young.

sawfish
A flat-bodied, cartilaginous fish related to sharks that has a long, sawlike snout.

skate
A flat-bodied, cartilaginous fish related to sharks and similar to a ray, except it lays eggs.

species
A group of animals or plants that have similar characteristics and are able to breed among themselves.

spiral valve
Corkscrew-shaped folds in a shark's intestine that help slow digestion.

squalene
An oil present in the liver of sharks.

swim bladder
An air-filled sac in many fish that helps them stay afloat.

tag
To attach a marker or label to a shark's skin to track its movements.

temperate
Describes places between the tropics and poles where there are distinct seasons.

tropical
Describes places close to the equator where it is hot all year round.

vertebrate
Having a backbone.

viviparous
Describes an animal that produces young that develop inside the mother's body.

zooplankton
Animal plankton.

Galápagos shark

Index

Acknowledgments

The publisher would like to thank the following for permission to reproduce their material.
Every care has been taken to trace copyright holders. However, if there have been unintentional
omissions or failure to trace copyright holders, we apologize and will, if informed, endeavor
to make corrections in any future edition.

Key: *b* = bottom, *c* = center, *l* = left, *r* = right, *t* = top, *bg* = background

Cover *c* Gary Bell/Oceanwide Images; *bg* Amos Nachoum/Corbis; Page 1 Alamy/Jeff Rotman; 2–3 Seapics/Bob Cranston;
4–5 Seapics/Phillip Colla; 7 Frank Lane Picture Agency (FLPA)/Norbert Wu; 8–9*t* Ardea/Valerie Taylor; 8–9*b* Seapics/Doug
Perrine; 9*tr* Seapics/Doug Perrine; 9*cr* Seapics/D. D. Schrischte; 9*br* Seapics/Jonathan Bird; 11*b* Seapics/David B. Fleetham;
12*b* Seapics/Mark Conlin; 13*t* Nature/Jeff Rotman; 15*c* Seapics/Doug Perrine; 15*br* Seapics/Bob Cranston; 16*tl* Alamy/Ace
Stock Limited; 16*tl* FLPA/Minden Pictures; 16–17*c* Seapics/Garry Bell; 17*tr* Seapics/Richard Herrmann; 17*br* Seapics/
Manfred Bail; 18–19*bg* Seapics/Paul Humann; 18 Seapics/James D. Watt; 19 Seapics/Stephen Kajiura; 20–21 Nature Picture
Library/Doug Perrine; 21*t* Seapics/David Shen; 21*b* Seapics/Doug Perrine; 22–23*t* Nature Picture Library/Doug Perrine; 22*b*
Nature Picture library/Jeff Rotman; 23 Seapics/Jeff Jaskolski; 24 Alamy/Mike Greenslade; 25*t* Seapics/Doug Perrine; 25*b*
Seapics/James D. Watt; 26–27*t* Seapics/Richard Herrmann; 26*b* Seapics/Amos Nachoum; 27*b* Seapics/Masa Ushioda; 28*tl*
Getty Images/Time & Life Pictures/Henry Groskinsky; 30*c* Photolibrary.com; 30*b* Nature Picture Library/Brandon Cole; 31*r*
Getty/Imagebank; 31*b* Photolibrary.com; 32 Seapics/Doug Perrine; 33 Photolibrary.com; 34 Seapics/Jeff Rotman; 35*tl*
Corbis/Louie Psihoyos; 35*bl* Nature Picture Library/Jeff Rotman; 35*br* Getty/National Geographic Society; 36–37*t*
Photolibrary.com; 36*b* Seapics/Doug Perrine; 38 Seapics/Doug Perrine; 39*tr* Seapics/Jeff Rotman; 39*b* Seapics/Ron &
Valerie Taylor; 40–41 Alamy/Stephen Frink Collection; 40*l* Science Photo Library; 41*t* Alamy/Bruce Coleman; 42 Nature
Picture Library/Alan James; 43*tl* Seapics/Peter Parks/iq3-d; 43*cr* Photolibrary.com; 44–45*t* Seapics/A&A Ferrari; 44*b*
Ardea/Valerie Taylor; 46 Seapics/Bob Cranston; 47 Seapics/Masa Ushioda; 48 Alamy/Visual&Written SL; 48–49 Art
Archive/Biblioteca Nacional Lisboa; 49*t* PA Archive; 49*b* Corbis/Canadian Museum of Civilization; 50*cl* Corbis; 50–51 AKG/
Disney Enterprises; 51*t* AKG/Universal Pictures; 51*b* Corbis/James Leynse; 52–53 FLPA/Minden Pictures; 53*t* Seapics/Masa
Ushioda; 53*b* FLPA/Minden Pictures; 54 Ardea/Valerie Taylor; 54*c* Sharkshield.com, Australia; 55*t* Nature Picture
Library/Peter Kragh; 55*b* Ardea/Valerie Taylor; 56*tl* Seapics/Andy Seale; 56–57*b* Nature Picture Library/Jurgen Freund; 57*t*
Corbis/Jeff Rotman; 58 Seapics/Jeff Rotman; 59*bl* Seapics/Doug Perrine; 59*tr* Werner Forman Archive; 60–61*t* Seapics/Masa
Ushioda; 60*bl* Photolibrary.com; 61*br* Photolibrary.com; 62–63 Photolibrary.com; 64 Seapics/C&M Fallows

The publisher would like to thank the following illustrators:
Ray Grinaway 45; Sebastian Quigley (Linden Artists) 14–15; Sam Weston and Steve Weston (Linden Artists) 28–29;
Steve Weston (Linden Artists) 10–11, 12–13; Peter Winfield 8, 10, 19, 24–25, 36, 37, 43.

EMMA S. CLARK MEMORIAL LIBRARY

SETAUKET, NEW YORK 11733

To view your account,

renew or request an item,

visit www.emmaclark.org

DEMCO